HOW TO BECOME AN AUTHOR IN JUST 24 HOURS

FASTEST GUIDE TO WRITE A BOOK

JITHENDER KUMAR

Dedicated to my family ♥

Contents

CONTENTS

This table of contents will help you to navigate the topic you want to quickly refer to...

FOREWORD

There is a need for spreading many inspiring stories to the modern world. Author Jithender Kumar believes sharing your story through book medium is one of the best way to convey thoughts in a beautiful way. And there are loads of young business owners, coaches and free lancers struggling to planning to remove some timie from their daily busy schedule to write a book but not able to complete their book on time.

So JK decided to give them an easy way to complete their book hastle-free template. This is one of the major reason to write this book and transform people's lives in million ways.

Vettri Vendan
Credentials
10-02-2023

Preface

I am so happy living my life today as a life coach, but in my coaching journey I could lot of people needed help in establishing their identity or sharing their story in a common platform. I myself was once a victim of the same.

I am an engineer, a post-graduate and manager by profession. I was thirsty enough to put my opinions, thoughts into my first book on achieving dreams. Glad lot of people could connect with me & believe me I could inspire and help atleast 25 others to write their own book.

It is a blessing to write a book on this self-help topic. All I use is a easy replication system method which anyone can follow. This is a practical guide which can help you write your book with high discipline and good confidence levels.

101% you will thank me once you complete reading this book.

I have made this book intentionally short, crisp & express version - so that you can save your time and more productive in writing your book to completion without break.

Happy Writing!

JK

Acknowledgements

I would like to thank my family who could spare me time while drafting this book.

I cannot forget to thank my fellow coaches and team members who work with all my clients day & night to produce this incredible system of writing a book in just 24 hours.

I would love to thank all the authors in this world who is still producing content and running this

BOOK INDUSTRY LIVE!!!

Grateful to god & another day of my life

JK

Prologue

You have a book idea, and you think it would resonate with enough people to justify putting the work into writing it. But you still have doubts.

So, you're asking yourself, "Should I write a book?

Well you are at the right place.

The book is about, how you can spread your story to the world by writing a book. This book will give you practical ideas and basic structure about how easily one can write a book.

As you read the book,

1. You'll learn more about yourself.
2. You'll learn how to write and self-publish a book.
3. You'll create a stream of passive income.
4. You won't have to regret not trying.
5. You'll come up with more ideas.
6. You'll stoke the fires of your creative genius.
7. You'll gain knowledge
8. You'll reignite a passion
9. You'll stop making excuses
10. You will feel proud.

So let's dive in to read this amazing book and write one book soon :)

-- JK

I

"The Book Market"

Today's book market talks about

- "It's not about what am I writing, it's about how I write"
- Jack & Field always said Book writing is all about

  I use this simple formulae:
  [Writing a book = 10% Content + 90% Everything]

- 90% includes (TITLE + BOOK COVER + REVIEWS)
- 90% will work when 10% is in place [Brand Element of the book]
- The Greater Purpose –

  – My purpose is to "Leave my Legacy Behind"
  What's your purpose?
  You need to know what is the purpose of writing your book.
  Some of the types of purposes could be:

- To Display Your Identity: "You will discover who you are."

By its very nature, writing is an introspective, thoughtful activity. The process of writing a book will force you to turn your thoughts inward. Through writing, you'll gain perspective about what really matters to you. Writing a book will also teach you about the unique value of your own willpower. The simple act of committing to a writing project, and seeing it through, will measure the depths of your discipline. Writing a book can be a powerful way to get in touch with your thoughts, values, and motivations. Plus, writing is cheaper than therapy!

- Maybe you are a born writer (You just feel like writing)

Everyone can be a writer. Each one of us has a story to share. In fact, most of us have more than one story to share. The simple truth is that in order to be a writer, you just need to write. And to become an author, you just need to publish what you write.

- You will pocket a healthy chunk of change.

The brilliant ideas you have kicking around in your head aren't earning you any money. Only once you commit those ideas to paper and hit publish will you earn income from your thoughts. Your book can earn you a stream of passive income simply by existing. And then there's the future—audiobooks, courses based on your book, and speaking gigs! And, that's just the tip of the iceberg. You can make money off your self-published book—but you need to write it first.

- Time here is finite.

Nobody's getting out of this life alive. Our time here is finite. It's our choice how we want to spend our time. If you've ever wanted to write a book, don't wait for a life crisis to force your hand. The time is now. You have a chance to share your words, thoughts, and passions with the world. Don't let that chance slip through your fingers.

- Discover WHY: You will reignite a passion.

Each one of us has a passion for something—whether that's rock-climbing, organic cooking, or comedic storytelling.

What's your passion? You already know the answer to that question.

Here's our next question: When's the last time you stoked that passion? If that answer is, "you can't remember" or, "it's been years," then you've got some work to do. You owe it to yourself to explore your passion and write a book. We promise that when you're writing about something you love, it won't feel like work.

- You will be a pro author.

Only 1% of the world's population ever publishes a book. That's a heady statistic. By writing a book, you set yourself apart from the masses. Even if your book is fiction or a Non-fiction, the fact that you're now an author lends an air of authority to your professional endeavors. You can now add "author" to your CV, LinkedIn, and professional website.

In short: No matter what you write a book about, becoming a published author boosts your professional authority.

You'll have accomplished something few other people have.

My preemptive greeting: Welcome to the JK's Book Writing Club!

I guarantee you'll like the rarified air up here.

- You will tackle a new challenge.

Life has so many obligations—taxes, school pick-up, miles on the treadmill—it can be easy to fall into a daily rut. Writing a book is leaving your comfort zone. Trying something unfamiliar can be scary—we get it. But, that's precisely why it's exciting. The only way you grow as a person is by forcing yourself to leave your comfort zone. Time to jump off the cliff—write a book and become an author this year. You'll be amazed at how much you'll gain by pushing the limits of your own self-imposed boundaries.

- You will gain more knowledge.

Writing a book requires research. No matter what topic you're writing about, you're going to have to research new concepts and topics. By opening the door to new ideas, you'll educate yourself on a broad array of ideas. You'll be invigorated by how much you learn while you're writing, and emerge much brighter for having done so.

And when you're done, you can assert yourself as an expert in your field. Your book can then open the door for speaking engagements, conference presentations, and other professional networking opportunities.

- You will stop making excuses and just do it.

We know, we know, you've been mulling over the idea of writing a book for months (years?) now. Otherwise, you wouldn't be reading this article.

How long are you going to give yourself permission to keep quashing your dreams? *(Source: Self-Publishing School)*

It's time to commit and just do it.

> *"Commitment is what transforms a promise into a reality."*
> *Abraham Lincoln*

If you are committed, then

Welcome once again to JK's Book Writing Club!

I found the easy technique and used the below book writing structure to help at least 25 Authors to write their books well within time and made them published successfully (Both paperback & kindle version)

My Book Writing Structure has below 10 Categories:

1. Fix a schedule and deadline
2. Proven step-by-step process of writing a book in 15 Days or less!
3. Know your purpose of writing your Book
4. Creating the Book Title and Sub-title.
5. Designing the Book Cover
6. Structure your Chapters
7. Editing your Manuscript
8. Publishing your Book
9. Setting the MRP of your Book
10. Guide to promote books in various social media platforms

Are you FINALLY ready to take action?

The only difference between an author and anyone else is the fact that they wrote the book. They started.

And you can start TODAY.

I had written my first book titled "Will I Ever Buy My Ferrari?" (Available on Amazon) and after helping at least 25 Authors to write and publish their books, this will be my 26th & more books to help you write a book :)

Snapshot of my First Book at Amazon Website:

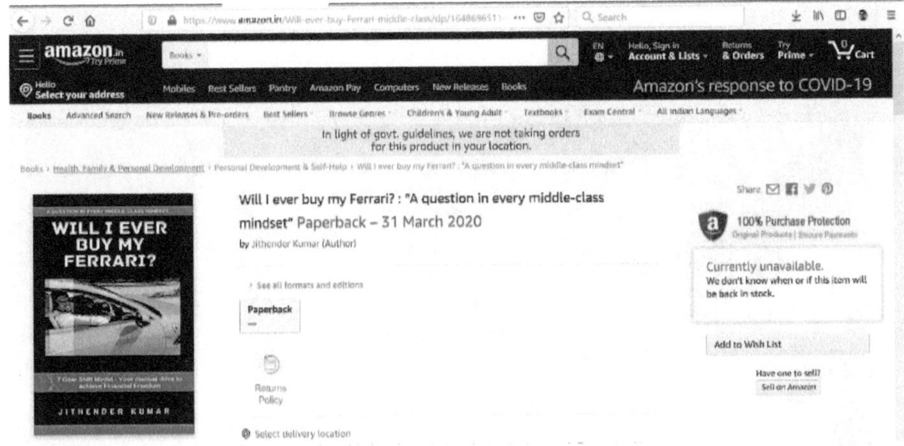

5 Star Rated Book :)

Similarly,
Your First Book should be displayed in below box soon:

Manifest Your Dream Book

The two Major Characteristics of a Writer – While writing a Book

1. You have to be the "Subject Matter Expert"

2. You should have an Intention in making people's lives better

<u>Subject Matter Expert:</u>

You need to know In & Around Your Niche

You need to have a thourough knowledge and study about your subject

Making People's Lives Better:

Its great, if your WHY is to help others voluntarily

It would be great, if your book can be a solution for someone around the Globe.

II

Why you need a book?

I could share from my experiences of helping others, few reasons could be

- Become an expert
- Personal Brand of Celebrity Status
- E.g., For an actor, there is a "Recall Value" (an actor always feeds his image to all his audience continuously to safeguard his/her identity through ads, social media & movies)
- "Most effective way to get leads"
- Book creates your ultimate business card
- Build your confidence to next level

An Expert

Ac Actor

Procuring Leads for your Business or Niche

Book can become your ultimate Business Card to get an easy entry to speak on a bigger platform

Build your confidence to next level!

III

What stops you from writing a book?

Editors revise others' writing by reading it and identifying any grammar mistakes or content errors, while writers create and publish pieces of work such as books, articles and essays. Knowing the difference between editors and writers is important to save time as a writer.

An editor is a professional who reads and revises others' writing. They might suggest plot or content suggestions. Some editors only revise technical errors, such as spelling, grammar or punctuation mistakes. Other elements that an editor might identify can include fact-checking or looking for style guide errors. Editors aim to match the voice and tone of the writer so that the changes they make or suggest align with what the author writes. They might suggest changes to the writer, or they could make the changes themselves. Editors can work with many types of writings, such as books, blogs or newspapers.

WE ARE NOT EDITORS here! So, let's be focusing only on WRITING!!! Moreover,

- "Quest to write a masterpiece" is the biggest challenge for anyone to start writing. I am talking about the perfectionist who is reading my book right here!

- If you think, I will write my book only if I have the perfect ideas, stories, book cover and perfect timing! SORRY! This is not going to work.
- The secret tip is just jot it down what comes on your mind! Get started! No one would like to read a book of a Perfect Author. Your audience will like you the way you are!

Success in writing a book is

"*Working smarter way & not the harder way*"

Hard Research + Smart Writing can take us to places in people's heart

Obstacles to Writing a Book (And How to Mitigate Them)

Here are the eight greatest obstacles we've found our Authors in JK Book Writing club face as they write their books:

<u>1. Fear</u>

One of the most difficult parts of writing a book comes before you put a single word on the page. Every writer I've ever met has faced fear and self-doubt.

How to overcome Fear?

Be brave (and find your team of people).

It's normal to feel fear as you start writing, and even more so to be nervous about sharing your writing. But having a team is one of the best things you can do to ensure you finish your book. Most people think they can write their books all on their own, without support and encouragement and accountability. And that's why most would-be authors fail. When you have the right team, they will encourage you when you feel self-doubt, they'll support you when you're stuck, and they'll tell you to keep writing when you feel like quitting.

If you don't have a team yet, you need one.

2. Finding Time to Write

Writing an entire book doesn't happen in a day. It takes a dedicated period of time, taking hours or weeks or even months. Of course, regular life won't conveniently pause for you to give you the time you need.

When I wrote my book, I realized finding the time to write was a challenge some days back. Life tended to get in the way. Setting daily word count goals and deciding in advance when I'd be able to write was really helpful. Having a book plan in place at the beginning was key to staying on track during days that I experienced writers' block or lack of motivation.

It might seem impossible to write a book when you have multiple major responsibilities weighing on you. But one of my Author Ayesha Shaikh from Dubai decided her dream of writing a book was worth weaving into her busy schedule.

She said, "I have an adult son with Autism, and elderly parents I care for, plus a full-time job. I had to find creative ways to get the writing done (at lunch, while waiting for my dad while running dirhams, late at night, whenever I had a few minutes to spare). There were times when I had to simply let them know that I had to work on my book."

Think you don't have time to write a book? The truth is, no one does. But if you want to write a book badly enough, you can find and make the time you need to get your story on the page.

How to find time to write?

If you want to write a book, choose to make writing a priority.

Look through your schedule and plan exactly when and where you'll work in your writing time. Maybe it's 5 AM at the kitchen table, five days a week. Maybe it's an hour at lunch, or after the kids go to bed. Maybe you'll need to sacrifice something to carve out time, like watching TV in the evenings. I woke up every day at 5.00 AM to write 5 pages of my book every morning.

Set your intention for your writing time. Then, stick to it.

Need more time? Look for gaps of a few minutes throughout your day: waiting in line at the grocery store or the doctor's office or the school pickup line. Pull out a notepad or your phone and jot down notes for what you'll write next when you're able to sit down with your story.

Yes, you're busy and you have no time to write a book. But you also have more time than you think. For as long as it takes to write your book, choose to make writing a priority and cram it in wherever it will fit.

Want more tips for finding time to write, even when you have no time?

(Email me at jkauthorsclub@gmail.com, 93568 38104)

3. Meeting Deadlines

Writing a book is an enormous undertaking. To break that into manageable tasks, these writers were given weekly deadlines. That didn't mean those deadlines were easy to meet, though. Here's what Anurag Saxena, author of the book HELL HEARTH, has to say about the experience of writing to a deadline:

"The most challenging part was getting my 6,500 words written before the "last minute" on Fridays. But I did it and met every deadline. This has given me great confidence."

Venkat, who finished her first book at the age of 59, realized quickly that if he wanted to meet his goal, he'd have to fight for it.

"Life goes on regardless of our goals. It was at times difficult to stay on track. Fortunately, I'm competitive and respond well to the constant support from your admin members behind the scene."

How to meet Deadlines:

The first step to meeting your deadlines is to set deadlines. I recommend setting a weekly deadline, including the number of words you're required to write each week and the day and time by which you'll need to write them.

But don't rely on your own willpower alone to ensure you meet them. Your willpower may be strong when you begin, but somewhere towards the middle, you'll hit a slump, and those deadlines will become harder and harder to meet.

To ensure you're successful week after week, find someone who will hold you accountable to meeting your deadlines.

Remember that team we talked about, the team that will help you overcome your fear? They'll also give you the tough love you need to fulfill your word count goal and meet your deadline every week.

As Venkat discovered, it would have been all too easy to miss a deadline, or two, or three when life got in the way. But with support, he was able to keep writing and finish his book.

4. The Perfect Author Syndrome

The book in your imagination is wonderful. Brilliant! Genius! Inspired! If critics could only read it right now, you'd be on the top of the India's Bestseller list, no question.

And yet, when you sit down to write, the words don't come out like you imagined. They're messy, unpolished, nowhere near that vision of the instant bestseller you're dreaming of.

Once I was writing epic fantasy, realized quickly that if I tried to write a perfect book on the first try, I'd never finish anything. It took time, but I managed to silence the voice of perfectionism and allow myself to just write, even when the words were a mess.

[The greatest challenge was] defeating the inner critic, or at least putting the critics call on hold. The first couple of weeks were tough. I think I have rewritten the first chapter four times now. But by week three I tamed that monster and started getting on with the book.

Perfectionism is tempting because it promises you that if you just work hard enough, polish each word before you type it, when you're done your book will be a work of genius. But the truth is, all first drafts are messy, and that's how they're meant to be.

How to overcome Perfectionism:

"Give yourself permission to write poorly."

Give yourself permission before you start to write. Give yourself permission again when you're excited, when the writing is flowing and every word seems perfect. Give yourself permission again when you're discouraged, when it seems like every word is a mess, and there's no hope for your story.

Remember, first drafts are meant to be messy. If your first draft is flawed, you're doing it right.

If your inner critic won't be quiet, hide your writing from yourself. Change your type font to white, or make it too small to read, so there's nothing to criticize.

Above all else, meet your deadlines. There's no time for perfection when you have 3,000 words due in six hours.

5. Finding Writing Tool

At the most basic level, the only tools you need to write are a pencil and paper. But if you want to keep track of an entire manuscript, it's helpful to take advantage of technology.

Supporting Tool:

The best book writing tool is the one that works for you. If typing is holding back your writing, try voice typing your story with a tool like Google Docs.

My favorite book writing Tool is Voice Typing. It's makes writers work easy, and it gives you the flexibility to break up your book into chapters and scenes so you can work with just a small piece at a time and easily reorganize anything. Snapshot is here:

This Voice Typing Tool had helped me & my fellow coaches alot! Do try once and share feedack!

Open a blank Google Doc = then go to Tools = then click = Voice Typing = "You can just hit the mic & speak – it will type of you" :) It's fun though!

6. Self-Discipline

It's all well and good to have a deadline. But deadlines are only effective when you do the work to meet them. And as Ayesha Shaikh found, that gets more difficult the deeper into your book you get.

During this whole process, about mid-way through actually, I remember sitting down at my computer thinking that I just can't do this anymore. But I committed to the process (the 10 days) and was determined to see it through to the end.

How to develop Self-Discipline?

You may have started writing your book because you had a brilliant idea, you felt deeply inspired, or you loved the act of writing and telling stories. While all those things are wonderful, they alone won't carry your story to the end.

You will experience slumps in the writing process. When they come, don't use them as an excuse to quit writing.

Rather than waiting for inspiration to return, write your way back to it.

Maybe you need to change up something in your writing process. Try writing in a different writing space, or at a different time, or by pen or dictation rather than typing it all up.

Maybe you need to revisit your plan, the idea that got you started, and reimagine the story.

Whatever you do, don't rely on your inspiration alone, or even your own self-discipline. Reach out to your team, let them know that you're struggling, and ask for support.

Then, keep writing until you meet your writing deadline.

7. Family Emergencies and Illness

One of the most difficult challenges an Author faces when writing a book is navigating the unexpected life events, family emergencies, and illnesses that are bound to happen over the course of a few months. Deadlines, goals, and self-discipline are vital, but sometimes family has to take priority.

One of my middle east authors Umair Faruq realized quickly that he'd need to adjust his expectations for himself and his writing, or he'd get discouraged and quit before he ever got going.

He said,

"I have chronic migraines, and have days, sometimes several in a row, when I can't write. Actually, when I can't get off the couch. At first, I felt like I was failing if I missed the Friday deadline, but I came to realize that if I was going to be a writer, I had to make peace with my limitations, accept that there were days that I had to view the deadline as a goal, not a contract, and post my submission a day or two late."

How to handle such unforeseen situations:

If you've ever experienced tragedy, a family emergency, or health problems like these, then you know how it can make writing a book feel inconsequential. What's the point of writing a book when you're in pain all the time? Or grieving the loss of a loved one?

How do you keep going? SHOULD you keep going?

If you're experiencing something like this, first let me just say, I'm so sorry. Second, it's okay if you need to take a break from writing for a while. But before you step back, here are a few things to do first:

Let your writing community in. Share what happened with your writing community. They are there to support you, not just with your writing but your life, too. You might find that they have gone through similar things and can help encourage you through your journey.

Use the pain or grief to fuel your writing. Some of the greatest writers in history have experienced huge amounts of trauma and suffering. The great Russian author Dostoyevsky was exiled to Siberia where he faced near-starvation. Ernest Hemingway lost his father at a young age to suicide. Instead of letting pain and tragedy impair their writing, they were fueled by it.

8. Reliving Personal Shock:

If you're writing memoir or basing your stories on your personal experiences, you face unique challenges. While I was writing my first book, I have had some good experiences and some bad. I decided to write this book to talk about my story and in the process overcome the pain I have endured in my journey. While writing is a cathartic process that helps to heal, writing about something that you are going through while it's still happening can be difficult. So, there were moments when I woke up in the morning and cried for hours, because the words I had put on paper made me more aware of the difficult road ahead of me.

How to overcome shocks:

When you write about trauma, it can feel like you're reliving that terrible experience, and while you might be tempted to avoid that, it can actually be one of the best ways to heal.

In one study, researchers found that people who wrote about their traumatic experience for as little as fifteen minutes had "significantly better physical and psychological outcomes."

In fact, many therapists prescribe writing as a way to heal from trauma.

Don't flee from your feelings. Write into them.

And if you're writing about trauma, don't feel like you have to share it with anyone, at least not right away. They are your experiences and your words. It's up to you what you want to do with them.

Your book plan can be as detailed or as sparse as you like. You can write extensive chapter summaries, or just a few sentences of synopsis. The important thing is to think through your entire book before you start writing, so you have an idea of what your story will be.

Of course, as Pat discovered, sometimes you have to be willing to throw out your plan. Your first draft is a process of discovery, and it's perfectly normal for your story to change and evolve as you write it.

Even so, taking time to think through your story will give you a boost when you find yourself in a slump. And when you get stuck, you'll be able to revisit those early ideas, develop a new plan, and keep writing.

Knowing about all these obstacles, how and where do we end of finish can be a challenge?

If you've come this far, that's amazing! With one final push, you'll make it to the end.

What do you need for that push? Here are a few strategies:

Figure out how much you have left to write. Are you just a couple scenes away from the end? Or do you have several chapters to go? Be honest with yourself about how much story is left in your book.

Reset your intention. Before you got started, you decided when and where you'd write. Revisit your intention and recommit to that plan.

Ditch perfectionism and be willing to experiment. Your ending doesn't have to be perfect. It just needs to be on the page. Give yourself permission to write a messy, weird, imperfect ending. It's okay! You'll fix it later.

Write faster. Struggling to make it to the end of your book? Challenge yourself to write faster. There's no time for perfection when you're writing in sprints.

(Credits: The Write Practice)

You Have What It Takes

Writing a book is a huge challenge. If you're wondering if you have what it takes, first know that you're not alone.

A few months ago, twenty-five writers started their books and most of them had this same question. Worse, it didn't go away as they wrote.

And yet, they finished their books. And so can you.

Maybe it's time to get started!!!

STILL NEED HELP IN WRITING A BOOK?

If you're thinking of writing a book, or if you've already started and are facing obstacles like these, I'd love to step into your corner and support you. We built the 10 Day Book program to help writers overcome all the obstacles that stop you from writing a book so you can finally finish.

Contact: jkauthorsclub@gmail.com, Mobile: 93568 38104

Instagram ID: @jklifecoach

10 Day Book is a transformational online program that will guide you through the book writing process. If you follow the process I teach you in 10 Day Book, you will have a finished book. Even better, you'll learn a process you can use again and again to write books in the future.

The 10 Day Book program is open for a limited time, and I'd love to see you inside.

IV
HOW & FROM WHERE DO YOU START?

1. Always manifest or brainstorm ideas about the Cover of the Book First

- Once you are clear with your purpose of writing or clear with the niche, you can start jotting down the taglines and one-liners of your stories on a piece of paper.
- You can write at-least minimum 10 One-Liners around your niche or your purpose and write it.
- Gaze at the board or paper, think of images related to those taglines. If possible, you can save few images in your laptop / phone / desktop.
- You will get a rough idea of what your book cover should be
- Have at least 4 to 5 types of images in your mind. We can definitely short-list one late

2. Choose the Title & Sub-Title of the Book

- Choosing a Title is like naming your new born baby or think of the words close to your mind and heart – listen to the inner critic's voice repeatedly saying few titles. This title has to match your purpose or the niche you planning to write about.

- Title can be short (maximum 2 words) but of course taglines can be catchy and have more than one line.

3. Create the cover of your book

- I personally use Canva app to design my book covers. I just love this app. It is very user-friendly and glass for your creative juices. Myself being a life coach, I spend at least 3 hours every day at Canva app. Canva app can be operated from Laptop as well. I have designed close to 350 book covers for authors. If you would want to get your book cover designed – Let me know!
- Make sure whatever images you place on the cover has to be copywrite free images. You can download copywrite free high quality images from www.pixabay.com or www.unsplash.com (both websites are more than enough!)
- Although I don't recommend as a mandatory procedure, but try to have one of your good quality face images placed on the book cover, this will help in establishing your initial identity in the book market.

4. Table of Contents

- How do you structure a table of contents?

To write a table of contents, you first write the title or chapter names of your research paper in chronological order. Secondly, you write the subheadings or subtitles, if you have them in your paper. After that, you write the page numbers for the corresponding headings and subheadings.

- The two things that should be seen in the table of contents are the names of the sections or chapters in the writing and the page numbers on which they are found

- What is the purpose of table of content?

The table of contents serves two purposes: It gives users an overview of the book's contents and information flow. It allows readers to go directly to a specific section of a specific chapter.

5. About the Book

- Average words recommended by me to write your first Non-fiction book can be somewhere around 15000 words to 30000 words length.
- What is a Non-fiction Book?

A Non-fiction Book is a literature that, regardless of the subject matter, has a simple goal: to provide information. It should be based on facts and conclusions of the author's research or expertise, as opposed to the creativity of the author's imagination. Granted, storytelling skills are required when writing a great work of non-fiction, but the content is still expected to be accurate. In addition to this, modern non-fiction is prose — writing that sounds like everyday speech and is not written in meter, like poetry.

- Types of Non-fiction Book:

    i. Histories
    ii. Biography, Autobiography, and Memoir
    iii. Science and Nature
    iv. Leadership and Self-Help
    v. Books about Current Affairs and Politics
    vi. Nonfiction Novels.
    vii. True Crime

I have always preferred writing on the category of Leadership and Self-Help Books because that supports my Life coaching profession.

These books are part of a long tradition of nonfiction that provides instructions for how to rise up and become your best self — whether in your personal or professional life. In Never Enough (2021), Mike Hayes distills the lessons he learned as a Navy SEAL commander and shows us how to use these tactics inside and outside the boardroom. In Talking to Strangers (2019), Malcom Gladwell demonstrates where we fail in our conversations with people we don't know, and how we can avoid the conflict this creates. In 2014, Marie Kondo famously taught the world how to graciously kick our clutter to the curb with The Life-Changing Magic of Tidying Up.

- How Many Books Does the Average Person Read?

George R. R Martin once said readers relive thousands of lives reading, while non-readers only live once. Americans have varied reading habits across different demographics. Some prefer to flip the pages, others listen to audiobooks, and for some, scrolling through an e-book is okay.

The average number of books each person read over the course of a year was 12, but the most avid readers inflate that number. The most frequently reported number was 4 books per year. Of course, there's plenty of variation among demographics.

The map below, reprinted in The Paris Review, shows that Indian people actually spend the most time in-between pages, followed closely by the Thai and Chinese. Americans are slackers compared to these countries, spending just a little more than half the time reading that our Indian counterparts do.

Indians at the top!

"CEOs tend to be Voracious Readers"

How much the average CEO reads?

Study says that executives read 4–5 books per month, far outpacing the general population. As for what they're reading, it's not all motivational or business-themed: many top CEOs also reported reading novels, plays, and philosophy.

As far as my experience is concerned, I tell my Authors,

"60% of books are not read to completion!"

WHAT IF YOU DON'T HAVE CONTENT?

That's a great question!

Almost many of you must have heard about the book titled "Think and Grow Rich" by Napolean Hill. I would like to mention the success secret of this book.

Think and Grow Rich is a book written by Napoleon Hill and Rosa Lee Beeland released in 1937 and promoted as a personal development and self-improvement book. He claimed to be inspired by a suggestion from business magnate and later-philanthropist Andrew Carnegie. However, there is no evidence that the two ever met.

The book is considered a classic in the personal development genre and has been widely influential in shaping the way people think about success and wealth.

Think and Grow Rich is based on Hill's earlier work The Law of Success, claims to be the result of more than twenty years of study of many individuals who had amassed personal fortunes. Hill studied their habits and drew some 16 "laws" to be applied to achieve success. Think and Grow Rich condenses them, providing the reader with 14 principles in the form of a "Philosophy of Achievement".

Point to be Noted: Hill never had his own content, he always interviewed some of the most rich people around the planet and identified the principles as the "13 Steps to Riches," which include developing a positive mental attitude, setting clear and specific goals, developing a plan to achieve those goals, taking action, and maintaining a strong belief in oneself and one's abilities.

Sharing a photo of Napoleon Hill holding his book *Think and Grow Rich - 1937*

Source: Wikipedia | This image is available from the United States Library of Congress's Prints and Photographs division under the digital ID cph.3c36395.

Image Link Source: https://en.wikipedia.org/wiki/Think_and_Grow_Rich#/media/File:Napoleon_Hill_holding_book_1937.jpg

<u>Image Link Source</u>: https://en.wikipedia.org/wiki/
Think_and_Grow_Rich#/media/File:Napoleon_Hill_holding_book_1937.jpg

The Key here is even if you don't have content, you can do these two things:

○ Take Interviews of ...

    i. People who became successful in your niche
   ii. Highly Successful Rich People (if you are writing a book on wealth)

- ○ Put their learnings in the book

You will be able to succeed in getting content and not left empty!

V
BOOK IS A BUSINESS!

1. Write your book, publish it in Amazon – Sell Online

Amazon went public in May 1997. It began selling music and videos in 1998, and began international operations by acquiring online sellers of books in the United Kingdom and Germany. Selling Books are in the DNA of Amazon's Business. So do try publishing your book through Amazon. Let me know if you need any help or assistance in publishing your book at Amazon or kindle version. (Reach out to jkauthorsclub@gmail.com or 93568 38104)

2. Write your book, release it in Notionpress – Sell Online

I released my first book through Notionpress publisher (India's #1 Publishing Platform) - Trusted by over 30,000 authors worldwide. I had a pretty good experience. Very user-friendly interface for beginners.

3. Make a video course on the same topic – Sell Online

If you have a YouTube channel or you can daily make 30 seconds video of your chapters (1 page a day – still you can make 100 videos – you can make it a Reel too @Instagram & @Facebook to build your identity)

We may not be able to travel all places over the world but our book or our videos can travel without a passport or visa :)

4. Make Audio clips, podcasts on same topic – Sell Online

I am a true fan of podcast. I podcast everyday morning 5.00 AM IST. I have my podcast channel @Spotify (JK's Joy Box) & @Apple Podcast.

I enjoy my podcasts because I just talk about content written in my book

I speak about various topic about my book, my niche & that way I keep my audience engaged. Let me know if you need any assistance if you are planning to podcast your episodes and go on AIR! :)

5. Same Content – Keep repeating to your Tribe (in Facebook, Linked In)

Tribe here means "Your Target Audience" – All you need to do is to invest time & sit, focus and jot down your thoughts and write 1 book. Later you can share the same content in various social media platforms to keep your audience engaged. That way you can develop as many as followers.

6. Important thing which sells is the topic.

"My silence never means I don't have nothing to talk, but it was important who were audiences and what was the topic."
— Ali Rezavand Zayeri

Choosing a topic is the first and maybe the most important step of the research and writing process! This step will determine the rest of your steps -- what your book flow is, what sources you use, and how to write your chapters. So, it's important to make sure you choose a strong and engaging topic.

All we know by now.

A topic is the most essential and critical element to start doing anything. A topic has the power to define your niche in just 1 word.

"So, choose your topic "wisely""

because that's the only thing which will sell.

What does book do to you?

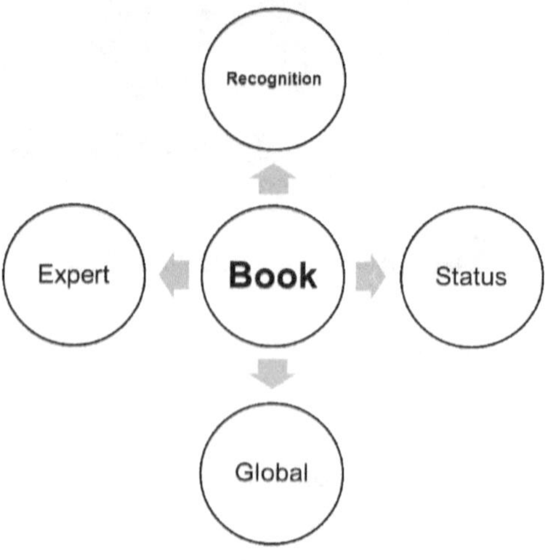

A book does :MAGIC: to you!

RECOGNITION:

As we spoke early, owning a book can give an identity that can separate from others. There are at times where you meet popular personalities may while travelling in a flight, imagine any cricketer or actors or popular youtuber is setting next to you, in such situations you may not have good time to tell about yourselves or share your story – but if you carrying your book – you can always take their autograph or hand over them your copy of book or if they allow – you can take a photo along with posing with your book – This will add credibility to your profile.

You would get recognized as Author in lot of Schools & colleges and Rotary clubs and make an easy entry to speak in their stages. You can become a speaker as well.

STATUS:

Book will be an added feather to your cap. You will get an additional Author status apart from your regular work. Makes you feel proud and better status symbol in the society you live in.

GLOBAL:

You and your story may not be able to reach the entire world so quick as much as speed of your book reaching the global audience. In today's world, there is a scarcity for true information, true story & authentic information. So why it cannot be your book reach the audience from a diverse global background. May be your book can provide solution to someone suffering on the other side of the planet.

Best thing about book is "You won't know who is reading through your book"

EXPERT:

In the journey of writing your book & researching a lot – unknowingly you become the book expert of niche expert or knowledge expert in that specific Zone. This expertise will further produce your confidence and plant more speaking or coaching sessions among your tribe. You become an SME (Subject Matter Expert)

VI
PURPOSE OF WRITING A BOOK!

My Purpose – My WHY!

1. "To reach people, create awareness and guide people to live a happy life"
2. "To "Leave a Legacy" – People might forget you who you go, but still they can read your book"
3. "Makes me Complete"
4. "Makes me Happy"
5. "Keeps me Creative"

What is your WHY?

If you don't know what is your purpose of writing – then there won't be any point in moving ahead!

An author's purpose is his reason for or intent in writing. An author's purpose may be to amuse the reader, to persuade the reader, to inform the reader, or to satirize a condition.

An author writes with one of four general purposes in mind:

1. To relate a story or to recount events, an author uses narrative writing.

2. To tell what something looks like, sounds like, or feels like, the author uses descriptive writing

3. To convince a reader to believe an idea or to take a course of action, the author uses persuasive writing.

4. To inform or teach the reader, the author uses expository writing. An author's purpose is reflected in the way he writes about a topic.

For instance, if his purpose is to amuse, he will use jokes or anecdotes in his writing. Clues to an author's purpose may be found in titles, prefaces, and the author's background.

Okay Let's have some fun while you are reading.

I will give you few exercises below. Read each paragraph. Then select the answer that best describes the author's purpose in writing.

Are you ready for the fun activity? – Take a Pencil & mark around the correct answer whatever you feel.

EXERCISE 1:

The word is terracide. It is not committed with guns and knives, but with relentless bulldozers, roaring dump trucks, and giant shovels like mythological beasts. Dynamite cuts and rips apart mountains to reach the minerals inside, leaving nothing but empty, naked hills. The land is left wasted and allowed to slide down upon houses and into streams, making the land unlivable and the stream water undrinkable. This is terracide, or if you prefer, strip mining.

1. The author's purpose is to

a. inform you about the purposes of strip mining.

b. describe a strip mining operation.

c. persuade you that strip mining is bad for the environment.

d. define terracide.

৪৩

EXERCISE 2:

The human sex chromosomes are of the XX-XY pattern. The Y chromosome is

much smaller than the X chromosome. Two types of sperm cells are formed during gametogenesis; half of these have the X chromosome and the others have the Y chromosome. Every egg cell has an X chromosome; therefore, fertilization determines the sex. If a Y sperm cell fertilizes the egg, a male develops.

2. The author's purpose is to

a. explain how the sex of humans is determined.

b. describe chromosomes.

c. tell the steps in fertilization.

d. contrast X and Y chromosomes

❧

EXERCISE 3:

To make a delicious New England pit, proceed as follows: take some water and

flour; then construct a bullet-proof dough. Make this into a disk-shaped object. Dry it for a couple of days in a mild temperature. Pour on stewed dried apples and slabs of citron; leave it in a safe place until it petrifies. Serve cold at breakfast and invite your mother-in-law.

3. The author's purpose is to

a. tell the steps in making a pie.

b. make fun of (satirize) New England cooking.

c. persuade the reader to buy New England pie.

d. describe New England pie.

❧

EXERCISE 4:

I will try to give the reader of this article some idea of the real nature of Gothic

architecture, not just of Venice, but of universal Gothic. One of the most interesting parts of our study will be to find out how far Venetian architecture went in achieving the perfect type of Gothic, and how far it fell short of it.

4. The author's purpose is to

a. explain the importance of Gothic architecture.

b. describe Venetian architecture.

c. show how Venetian architecture is different from Gothic architecture.

d. show the nature of Gothic architecture.

❧

EXERCISE 5:

On September 23, a large cavalry troop from Fort Robinson arrived at the camp of Sitting Bull. Just as he was about to give a welcoming speech, a commotion broke out among the watching warriors. Rifles were fired, and the meeting ended in a massacre of the soldiers.

5. The author's purpose is to

a. describe Sitting Bull's camp.

b. persuade the reader that the Indians were bloodthirsty.

c. tell the events leading to a massacre.

d. explain the problems of the Calvary.

EXERCISE 6:

Tofu is a product that is becoming very popular as a low-calorie, cholesterol-free

meat substitute. Formerly it was found exclusively in Oriental markets and health food stores, but today tofu can be purchased in most supermarket produce departments. This white, cheese like substance is made from the condensed milk of soybeans. It is extremely high in protein and low in sodium. Tofu is almost tasteless by itself, but it can be easily mixed into sauces and soups; it can even be made to imitate scrambled eggs.

6. The author's primary purpose is to

a. evaluate Oriental cooking.

b. persuade you to eat low-cholesterol foods.

c. describe tofu.

d. to compare tofu with meat.

EXERCISE 7:

Dear Tall, Dark and Handsome — This is your lucky day! The girl of your dreams is just a phone call away. I am 5' 10", slim, pretty, and only 23. I love pop music, good books, exotic foods, and foreign travel. Give me a ring any day after 6 P.M. You won't be sorry. Your gal, Jackie.

7. The author's purpose is to

a. convince the reader to call the writer.

b. describe the writer objectively.

c. criticize the writer's lack of intelligence.

d. entertain the reader with some interesting facts.

EXERCISE 8:

Our criminal justice system today is a disgrace. Modern day criminals have more

rights than an honest citizen ever imagined were written into our U.S. Constitution.

Murderers and rapists are typically set free on legal technicalities and seldom face any jail time. While that scum is back to work finding new victims, the pleas of those they have killed, maimed, or violated go unheard. Until we begin giving some real consideration to people who obey the law, instead of those who break it, things are going to continue getting worse.

8. The author's purpose is to

a. describe the actions of the criminals.

b. compare criminals with honest citizens.

c. inform the reader about the extent of crime in America.

d. criticize our criminal justice system.

Hope you had fun doing above activity. I coach my team this way! :)

Purpose of writing a book can be many

- Write because no one has time to listen and you might have a story to tell - and the joy of writing. What a platform. I know someone who wrote a book dedicated to a lost friend. Not a best seller but was so touched by the effort and the reason.
- It can be same as breathing for some people - lot of writers wrote as that's all they wanted to do.
- Its lucrative for some - good publisher, a mass appealing subject, one best seller can do wonders. This is a later stage.

Do read about lives of writers or artists.

Some were even very poor, motives are many. For writing a book.

One you know your WHY – 3 ideas to keep in mind!!

1. Who am I?

   ◦ Who will relate to me?

2. Who are you?

   ◦ Whom do you wish to target?

3. Forget about who are you

   ◦ Just decide which market to enter (Go Market Focused)

""A Book is not Written, it is ENGINEERED""

4 Parameters to consider!

What is the MAIN PURPOSE ...?

Who is the TARGET AUDIENCE ...?

Identify NEEDS/DESIRES/PROBLEMS (NDP)

Lets Write it !!

4 Vital Parameters to consider!

PARAMETER 1:

We have seen what your purpose should be and how to derive one.
We will be moving to the next chapter discussing a bigger topic that is

PARAMETER 2:

"Who is the TARGET AUDIENCE?'

Virtual Imagination: Your Target Audience

If you write a book without knowing your target audience, there are higher chances where you might end up writing a book for yourself. This is all fine and good unless you want other people to want to read your book. To know who your book is for, you need to know your target audience.

A target audience is who you write your book for. It's the group of people who would be the most helped or entertained by your book. Your readership might extend past your intended target audience, but the target audience is who you intentionally aim for.

In a typical non-fiction book, your target audience is who the book would help the most. Where a lot of new writers go wrong with this is when they write the book for themselves instead of for their audience.

For example, if you're writing a book about life coaching–a book with YOU in mind might just be a diary documenting your personal experiences being a coach. Unless you're already a celebrity, the audience for a book like that is likely you, your parents, and maybe your own book club if you guilt them into it.

A book by the same writer with the AUDIENCE in mind might be something like Best System for Life Coaching–people who are struggling to coach are now interested in your book. Now you've got a niche target demographic–new beginners of coaching Industry.

Narrowing your target audience before you write the book can help you aim for the content your readers will be most interested in. It also makes your book easier to sell.

TARGET AUDIENCE MATTERS!!

You want to know your target audience to know how to craft your book, how to pitch your book, and how to promote your book.

Try creating a profile for an imaginary virtual reader.

Answer these below 9 questions to find your book's target audience:

1. **How old are they?**
2. **What do they do for a living?**
3. **What media do they read and watch and listen to?**
4. **Are they single? Married? Cheating on their boyfriend?**
5. **Did they go to college? Did they graduate? What was their major?**
6. **Where do they live? How long have they lived there?**
7. **Favorite color? Favorite food? Favorite thing to do on the weekends?**
8. **What are they struggling with?**
9. **What do they want to change about themselves or their life?**

"Your virtual reader is representative of the average person in your target audience"

When you have your virtual reader, you have a clearer picture of WHO you're writing for. If your book is a knife, your virtual reader is the grindstone to sharpen it.

People who are interested in you, your advice, or content you produce, are probably pretty similar to people who would be interested in your books.

One of my tips for establishing your brand is by asking your existing network to list the three things they associate you with the most. This exercise can help to determine your target readership as well.

Also consider asking your network what THEY are into. What are their top three areas of interest? What kind of books do they already read? What is something they're currently struggling with, or have struggled with in the past?

Determining and narrowing your target audience will help with every aspect of book production, from writing it to selling it. Gather data, ask questions, and determine who has the most to gain from reading your book.

LOOK FOR BOOKS THAT ARE SIMILAR TO YOURS

Take the time to research other books that would be in the same category, genre, or niche. Search for 'established' and 'top-selling' books within the category and make a list of the titles and authors. Once you recognize who your competition is, it may be easier for you to pinpoint your potential readers because chances are, you share the same target audience.

DEEP DIVE AT SOCIAL MEDIA

Now that you have identified the established and top-selling books within your genre, look at who is following them on social media. Don't be surprised how much information can be gained by looking at the interactions and posts. Keep an eye out for the demographics, trends, and other habits that might not be obvious, but can provide a tremendous amount of useful information.

Another strategy for social media is to connect with groups and online communities that have shared interests. Run a search on Facebook for groups who are interested in books similar to yours. Look for followers for your book's genre on Twitter by searching for tweets that contain related hashtags. Carve out some time each day to work on these strategies.

SEEK FOR HELP

If you're having trouble identifying your target audience, ask other authors or industry professionals for help. Most authors would love to help a fellow author identify their target audiences and share knowledge. Make sure you 'pay it forward' when an indie author is looking for guidance from you. This keeps the book industry thriving.

Once you find your target audience, the focus shifts to building a following. There are a couple of ways to do this. First start with creating and sharing well thought-out content appropriate for your audience. Figure out the right times and platforms to post the content. Use software to automate and track your post schedule. Be generous with your time and thoughtful promoting others. Promote your message and book no more than 20% of the time. The other 80% should consist of promoting others along with tips, quotes, and content relevant to your message.

Once you're posting consistently, reach out and follow others aligned within your target audience. With more activity on your social media platforms, you should have more success with others following you back. Connect with like-minded people and promote each other. Go beyond just following or liking their profiles. Retweet or repost relevant content and connect with their followers as well. Find groups, organizations, and associations to help you be successful. You never know who will help you reach the next level of success.

PARAMETER 3: IDENTIFY NEEDS / DESIRES / PROBLEMS (We call it NDP)

Decide what your readers know or think they know about your subject.

To help you answer this question, ask yourself, "What is the probable source of their knowledge? Is it a direct experience or an observation? Will my readers react positively or negatively toward my subject?"

Next, ask yourself "What will my readers expect from my writing?"

When you are planning your writing, decide what your audience should expect to learn or gain by reading your essay.

You also need to consider how you can interest your readers in your subject.

If your audience is hostile toward your subject, decide how you can convince them to give your writing a fair reading. If your audience is sympathetic, decide how you can fulfill and enhance their expectations. If your audience is neutral, decide how you can catch and hold onto their attention.

Finally, you should decide how you can help your readers read your writing.

The structure of your paper can make your paper easy or difficult to read. Decide what kind of organizational pattern will help your audience see your purpose. Also, decide what guideposts and transitional markers your audience will need in order to follow your organization. Finally, decide what and how many examples your audience will need in order to understand your general statements.

Identify what problems you faced in your life and have sorted it out. If you have found a way to sort it out, then you should narrate the problems with solution in the form of real time stories wherein people would love to get connected with you!.

PARAMETER 4:- LET's WRTIE IT!!

Now we have discussed enough on the above 3 parameters, now let's take a pen or laptop or a mobile phone and just keep writing as we have got much more clarity than before. #ACTIONTIME

ॐ

VII
ACTION MODE ON!!!

This is my favorite mode because this mode not jut need your ideas but it would your discipline and dedication more!

Here we will be doing all the crafts and arts activity.

1. Use MS Word Format (Font Size of 8/9/10) & Font I prefer – "Bookerly"
2. Always think of writing 1 "page"
3. Make a list of 10 major categories (out of the NDPs of the Target Audiences)
4. To step into the shoes of your Target Audiences, please make a list of FAQs

    ◦   (write 5 to 15 questions per category)

5. Pick 1 question & answer them

    Answer can be of a paragraph containing stories of people, clients …etc…
    Pictorial Way of the skeleton should look like
    PAGE FORMAT…

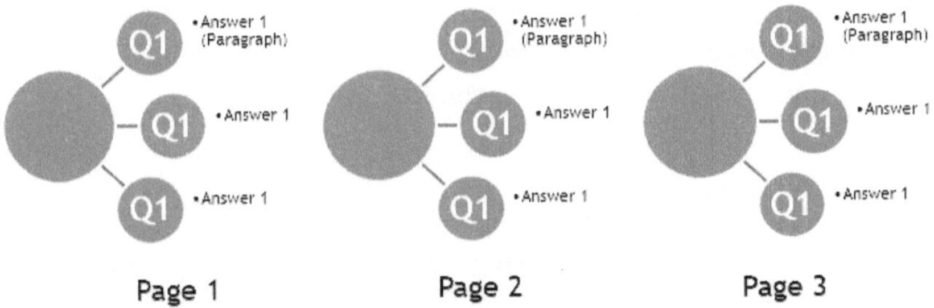

Page wise - How you can visually think of...Jot down your ideas in this format

CHAPTERS FORMAT...

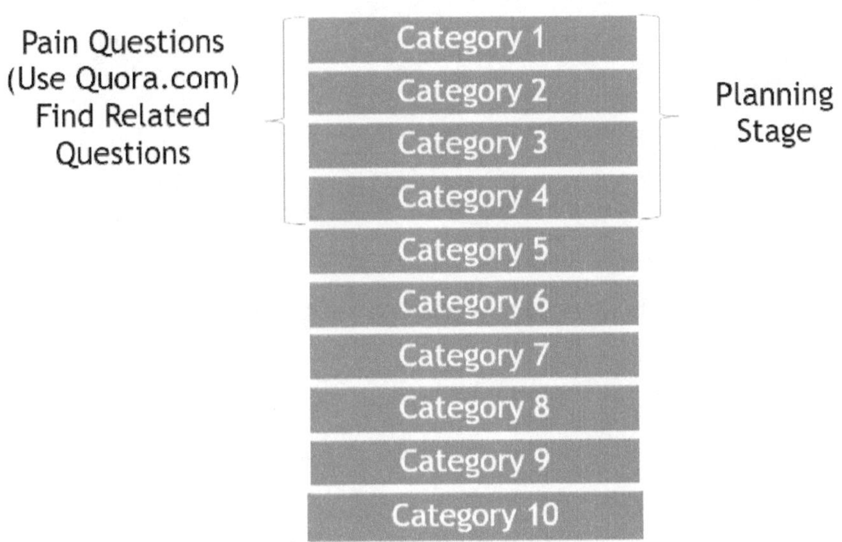

10 Chapters You Can Draft This Way!

Quora.com is an amazing garden to get more realistic and live knowledge from people around the world. You can place a question or you can search for answers to your questions, people would have already shared their answers there. You can find out your pain questions there as well.

That way write 5 questions in each category and answer them with your stories, client stories or friends stories, facts and life examples and events you will end up writing a great manuscript.

So, your book pages will roughly look like this...

Book Pages Template...

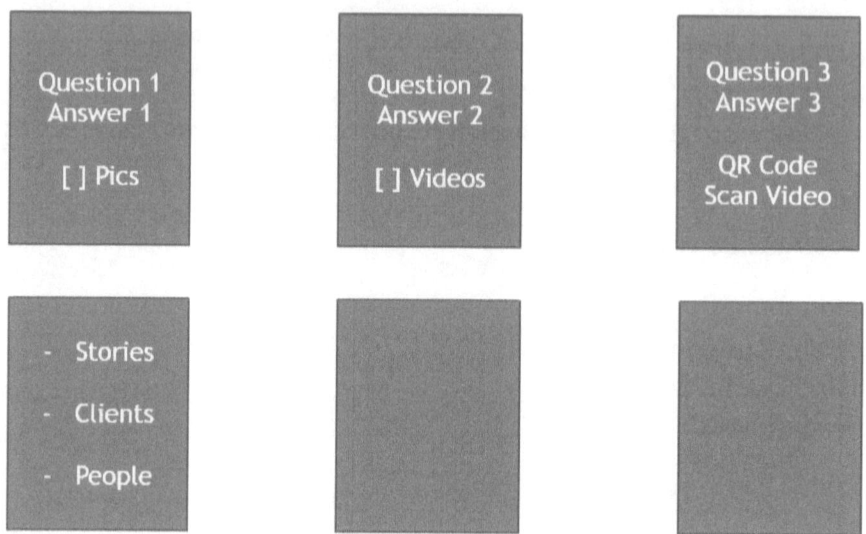

This way - you can do a structured approach!

1 Page – Pictorial Representation

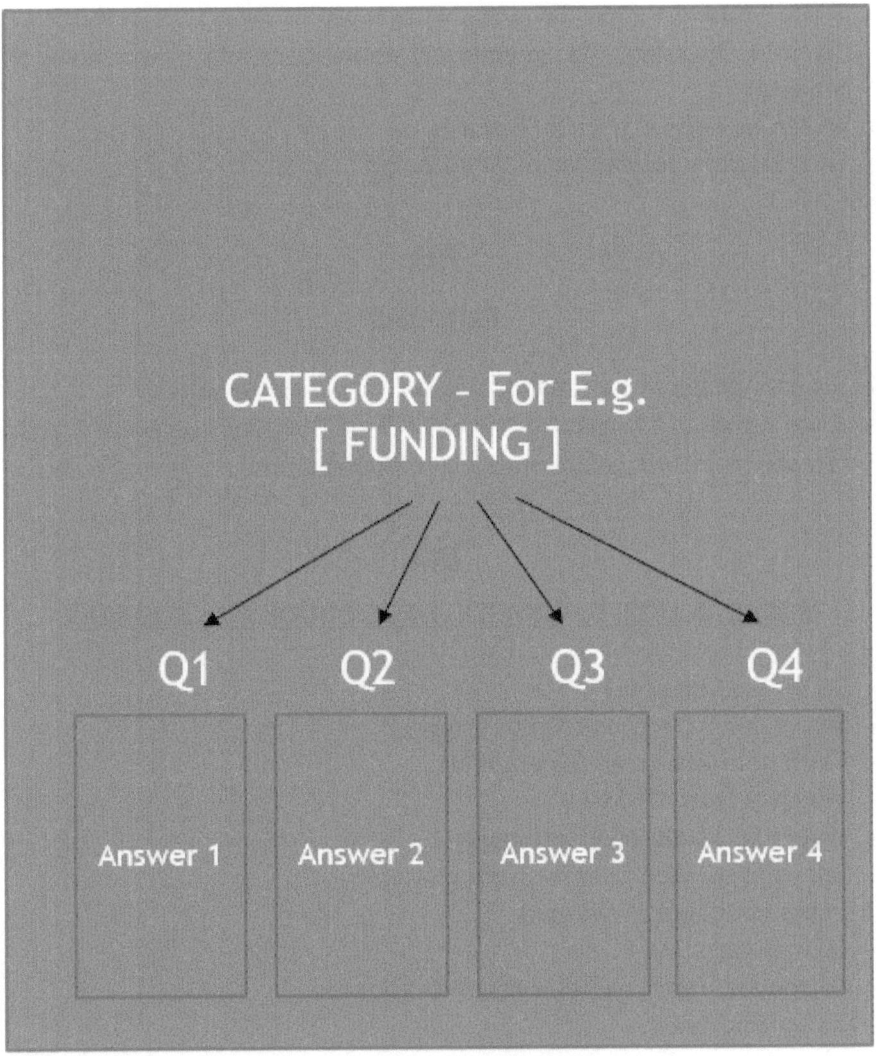

Example, if you are writing on the topic - Funding - We can have set of Q's this way!

This way you can keep building chapters and pages (No limits).
This we call it as **Ripple Model** or **Replication Model**.

<u>**SECRET HACKS TO COMPLETE YOUR BOOK MUCH FASTER**</u>

- 100 Answers / 5 per day = 20 Days
- Write 5 Answers every day = You will get 100 Answers (100 Questions)
- "Write 1 Question" that your target audience would like to know the answer
- In 2 mins = you can write 50 words
- In 10 Hours = you can write 15000 words

ॐ

Rule 5-10-5

- Read **5** e-Books, Watch **10** Videos & Scan **15** Search Results
- Go to Amazon – Search top 5 Books – Read their Reviews & see Ranking (This way you will get to know a lot of information)

ॐ

SECRET HACKS TO COMPLETE YOUR BOOK MUCH FASTER

- Go to "Youtube.com"
- Search for Top videos on your category
- Check for likes, views & comments
- Watch at-least 10 Videos
- Watch TED Talks on your topics
- See what speakers speaks on your category
- Put in your book if required
- Go to Google.com
- Search for "Top 15 websites result on your topic"
- Put in your book

This way you will not be left alone without any help. You will be able to write quickly & reach your Target audience closely. And mostly I would like to share an important tip here.

"DO NOT REVISIT 1ˢᵗ CHAPTER"

"*DONOT WAKE UP THE PERFECTIONIST TIGER SLEEPING INSIDE YOU!*"

Every Answers can be...
    Stories (Own)
    Stories (Friends)
    Stories (Clients)
    Interview Learnings
    Value Addition to the reader
    +
    Add Quotes
    +
    Add Statistics

Once you do this, we will end up in creating a Book content tree with all categories.

The skeleton of your book tree would look like...

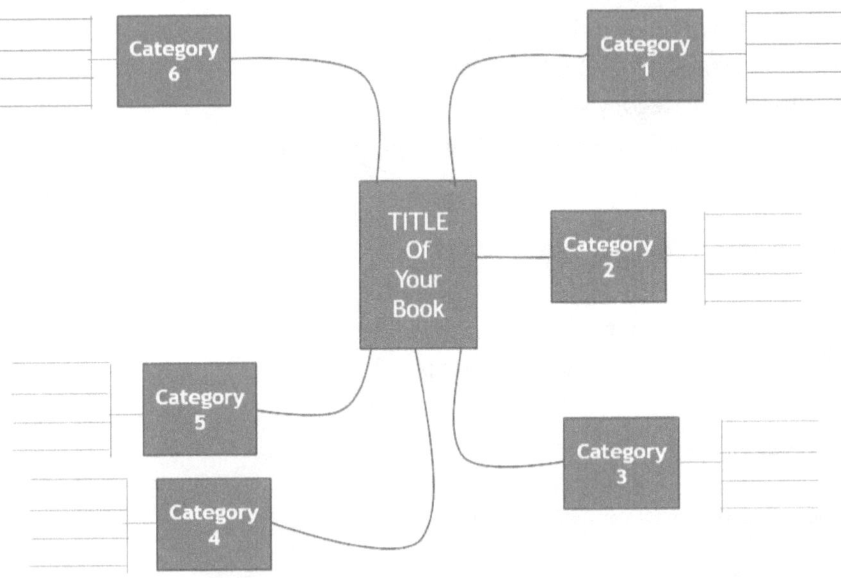

I call it as a "My Book Tree" - Seed, Water, Grow & Reap the Fruits :)

This chart you can roughly fill it with brainstormed ideas and take a print out and paste it on the wall like a checklist. That way you will be able to complete in a structured approach. You will also have a better flow.

VIII
Final Draft - Manuscript

There will be a difference between your first draft & Final Draft
  1 change, 2nd changes & 3rd edition becomes the final DRAFT.
  First Draft – Try to write 40,000 words
  This draft will go for elimination of {duplicate & repetitive content}
  Final Draft will have 20,000 words
  Write every category = Average of 2000 words
  10 Chapters = 20,000 words = That will make 1 Book

Thumb Rules…to keep in mind!

i.   "You buy books that you are familiar with"
v.   If you get 100 + Reviews on Amazon = then book sells on its own.

- Pricing of your book: -

- Keep Pricing between 300 to 400 INR Rupees

  (For 15000 to 20000 words book)
  Roughly 150 to 180 pages

- Always MRP of book = Double of its printing cost
- Editing cost in the market = 0.80 INR / word
- 80 paisa per word

For greater editing purpose of your manuscript, use software called **"Grammarly"**

Once book is published, go to "teachable.com" – Create a "free video course of your book" – So that your book reaches the market audience.

This one quote below which is always in my mind ensures every time you start writing a book, you will have a head start and be unstoppable!!!

ॐ

""DOUBT KILLS MORE DREAMS
THAN FAILURE EVER WILL !!""

Happy Writing!
Thank you & Best Regards,
JK - Your Life Coach

ॐ

EPILOGUE

If you need further help in writing your book, you can reach out to me and my team here at,

Name: Jithender Kumar R

Email ID: jkauthorsclub@gmail.com

Phone Number: +91 93568 38104

Place of Residence: Pune, India

Thank you & Good Luck!

JK – LIFE COACH

Do Reach Out for any Help! See ya Soon!